Piece of Time

Carrie Allen McCray

Chicory Blue Press, Goshen, Connecticut

A Crimson Edge Chapbook

Chicory Blue Press
Goshen, Connecticut 06756
© 1993 Carrie Allen McCray. All rights reserved.
Printed in the United States of America

Book Designer: Virginia Anstett

Some of these poems first appeared in *The South Carolina Collection,* an anthology of the South Carolina Writers Workshop, and in *Point,* an alternative South Carolina newspaper.

My appreciation goes back to my mother who encouraged us to read poetry – first, *A Child's Garden of Verse,* then works of the Harlem Renaissance poets. To my sisters, Rosemary and Dolly, my brother, Hunter, my niece, Elberta, and many friends for their encouragement. To my friend, Annie Laurie, who suggested I send some poems to Toi Derricotte, the first poet I dared send anything to and to whom I owe much for her criticism and encouragement. To the South Carolina Writers Workshop which motivates me. To Galway Kinnell and Sharon Olds of Squaw Valley Community of Writers, for opening up the closed doors in my head. To Sonia Sanchez, Nikki Finney, Laurence Lieberman, Lucille Clifton, Susan Ludvigson, Cornelius Eady, Robert Hass and C. K. Williams for their sensitive criticism and encouragement. To E. J. Laino for suggesting Sondra read my poems. To Sondra Zeidenstein for believing in my work and to Suzanne Wenzell, who not only types for me, but inspires me through her enthusiasm.

Library of Congress Cataloging-in-Publication Data

McCray, Carrie Allen, 1913-
    Piece of time / Carrie Allen McCray.
       p.   cm. – (Crimson edge chapbook)
   ISBN 0-9619111-4-X (pbk.) : $7.95
    1. Afro-American women – Poetry. I. Title. II. Series.
PS3563.C35249P54   1993   93-13496
811'.54–dc20   CIP
                                                        AC

Table of Contents

Reality   1
Nobody Wrote a Poem   2
I have a poem inside me   3
Red Balloons   4
My Father   6
Strange Patterns   8
My Grandmother's Leg   9
Thoughts at the Grave Site   12
Do White People   13
Trade-offs   14
Sixty-some Years   15
Back Home   16
Recycled Grief   17
I take my text from…   18
Harvesting   20
Piece of Time   24

Afterword   26

For my son, Scott – whose early creative spirit stays with me.

Reality

Four years old, and my mother,
with silken cover,
takes my hand and
thick tangled hair
to the Poro lady
a long day in hot-comb
hair-greased rooms
But I return home
with curls, and shake
them now like my
sisters,
And then – rain

Note: *Poro* is the brand name for grease used to straighten hair.

Nobody Wrote a Poem

Nobody wrote a poem
about me
In ugly tones they
called me "Yaller Gal"
How lovely to have been
born black or brown
Pure substance the artist
could put his pen to
Not something in between –
diluted, undefined, unspecific
I search the poets
for words of me
Faint mention in Langston Hughes'
Harlem Sweeties, I think,
yet I'm not sure
So full of "caramel treats,"
"brown sugars" and "plum
tinted blacks," it was
Soft, warm colors
making the poets sing
I, born out of history's
cruel circumstance,
inspired no song
and nobody wrote a poem

I have a poem inside me

I have a poem inside me
that refuses to come out
Someone told me a long time
ago
write a poem about your
husband and your marriage
For two years I've tried
to give birth, poem after
poem shifting in front of
this one, blocking its way out
"I am the writer in the
family," he used to say
controlling my pen as he
did all else
Is there now some
supernatural power he has
over me, holding back this poem
His home was Charleston
where some still believe in
the old "Hag"
Has she silenced my muse
I've been in labor many
times
One aborted, one breech,
one stillborn
I'll try again, I want
to birth this child

Red Balloons

Flapping signs read
Gray's Dixie Carnival
Papa, could I have one of
those red balloons
My sister, innocent at five,
did not know what she
was asking – but Papa did
That wonderful world
of merry-go-round,
red balloons dancing in the hot
southern breeze,
songs of summer in his eyes,
he risked it anyway,
stopped the car, went over
to the carnival gate
Could he just have a red
balloon for his little girl
The words of the carnival
man as hard as his face
"Nigger ain' nuthin here
for you or yourn"
Shaking her blond curls
a little five-year-old
stuck her tongue out
at Papa
Papa stood for a moment
then back to the car
with promises of lots of

red balloons when we get
home
I was eight years old then
but even now, whenever I
hear the sound of carousel,
I see Papa's wintered face
as he watched all the other
fathers
taking their children
through the gate

My Father

        I never saw my father in anything but a business suit. As if, after achieving, he could not let go. His hands washed, compulsively, scrubbing away some secret sin? or soot from rough laboring years.

        Born of that first generation out of slavery, he worked hard to send himself through school. A brilliant man in a long line of firsts. One of the turn-of-the-century Blacks to finish Michigan Law School. A good man, deacon in the church, superintendent of the Sunday school.

        A good father, caring, coming home with big bags filled with bananas, peanut brittle and coconut candy. But I never could run to him and hug him. Those business suits, starched white shirts and clean hands prohibitive to a small child.

        A protective father, he watched our development. I, coming late to early signs of womanhood, each month my father would ask "Miss Bussy, have you been unwell?" Always the picture of health – I did not understand. "No, Papa, I'm fine." Embarrassed later when I realized what he meant.

        When we were old enough to have company, young men would come to see us in groups. At nine o'clock sharp, my father would come to the top of the stairs and in the same voice used in court that day, call down: "Time for the young men to go to their homes now." The exodus immediate. All of our suitors called him *squire*.

I wanted something different of my father. Something our mother gave us. She loved working in her flower garden, would get down in the soft, wet squishy soil after a rain, make mud pies with us or let us plant her nasturtiums and phlox. She loved the feel of the earth, died with some under her fingernails.

I wanted my father, just one time, to take off that business suit, sit with us like Mama, let the wet soil roll around in his hands, squish it through his fingers, get his hands so dirty, he could not get them clean for a long time. Just once, just once is all I wanted. I would have run to him.

Strange Patterns

When I was a young child
in Lynchburg, Virginia
I could not ride the
trolley car sitting next
to our white neighbor
But could sit, nestled
close to her
under her grape arbor
swinging my feet
eating her scuppernongs
and drinking tall, cold
glasses of lemonade
she offered us on
hot, dry summer days

When I was a young child
moving to Montclair, New Jersey
I could now ride the
trolley car sitting next
to our white neighbor
but did not dare
cross the bitter line
that separated our house
from hers
and she never offered us
tall, cold glasses of lemonade
on hot, dry summer days

My Grandmother's Leg
A love story and an awakening

She would sit on the long, low porch on Holbrook Street in Danville, Virginia, wait for courting couples to pass, then call out "Come on, come on in, sit in the swing, I have a cool, fresh pitcher of lemonade." That was my Aunt Maggie, a wiry, cheerful, chattery old maid, gathering up her audience for her stories. Her stories always beginning with "before Mama lost her leg" or "after Mama lost her leg" as if her life were divided into two long seasons. I never understood this until the summer of my sixteenth birthday.

As we did every summer, when school was out, we went to Virginia to visit Grandma and Aunt Maggie. The train ride, a happy time, not too memorable the ride from Newark to Washington. But once on the Southern out of Washington, a picnic in motion. A car full of Black folk having their good time, shoe boxes on the racks loaded with fried chicken, pound cake and bananas. A communal people, everyone sharing, singing, laughing. The clickety-clack, clickety-clack of the train like a jazz beat faster, faster, faster. Clickety-clack, clickety-clack, clickety-clack. Taking us "back home."

And back home a round of dinners, parties, picnics and more dinners. As if to celebrate the return of the prodigals. Our trip usually ending with the big Baptist Sunday school picnic. This year everyone went except Aunt Maggie, always at the call of Grandma, and me because I did not feel well.

The house was silent, only an occasional call, "Mag, Mag, come my leg hurts." Aunt Maggie went to take care of her, then came back. "It's always the leg that's gone, bothering Mama. Never woulda lost that leg if we hadn't been in the Jim Crow car and that trunk came hurlin' out the baggage car, long time 'fore they came to see 'bout us in the Jim Crow car. Hospital turned Mama away in the Jim Crow town." I didn't know how to respond so said nothing.

After awhile, Aunt Maggie went to check. "Mama asleep now," she said. "Come on, baby, let's go over into the parlor." No one went in Grandma's parlor except on Sunday, so I knew this was special. We walked into the musty, red velvet room. Aunt Maggie did not open the blinds, went over and turned on the lamp with the rose-colored glass globe. Still dark in there. A sense of mystery. Then Aunt Maggie went over to the table in the corner, took a wooden box, tied with a blue ribbon, out of the drawer. "Here, baby," she said, "my eyes bad, read these for me," handing me a stack of letters. The paper so old it was brittle. Strange address on the envelope.

I opened the first one. "Dear Miss Mag," it said, "when I was at the mission tonight I thought of you and wished you were here as my wife like we planned. What a comfort you would be to me and to these poor suffering people of Africa…I know you have your calling there with her. God bless you for it." I read all the letters, each one speaking of his love for her, ending with – "And I remain respectfully yours, the Reverend Authur Moten." I finished the last one with a feeling of being back in a time when I was not. His presence so strong here, the Reverend Authur Moten.

I watched Aunt Maggie take the letters, place them gently in the box, tie it with the blue ribbons, quickly brushing tears from her eyes. Anger welled in me. At sixteen, romance is paramount to all other conditions of life. How could Grandma keep her away from him.

Then I thought of my grandmother who always said about her leg – "That ain' the worse trouble I knowed. Slavery done took more than a leg from me." My anger did not belong here, but I didn't know where, so just left it hanging without a target.

Summer over. Time to go home. Cousin Winslow drove us down to the train. Papa got on first, seated all of us in front of him. The train moved out slowly, then faster, faster, faster. Clickety-clack, clickety-clack, clickety-clack. The sound crushing into my skull. I leaned my head against the window. The vision of Aunt Maggie standing out in the street, alone, waving us goodbye would not leave me. And it was at that moment I knew.

Thoughts at the Grave Site
October 1935

All I could see
was you in your
red felt hat
walking briskly
out the front door
on the way to
the "fight"
you, who integrated
the living in our
small town
being lowered now
into a segregated
corner of the
graveyard

To my mother, longtime fighter
for equality and justice

Do White People

Do white people say
when there's a crime,
I hope he's not white
I doubt it

The newspaper blares:
"Armed men hold up gas
station, kill attendant"
Oh! God, please don't let
them be Black
And we search frantically
to find the signs that
tell us

    William Johnson – *Oh! Lord*
                Name sounds Black
    James Jackson – *Do Jesus,*
           must be

But do white people
Albert Lethington, tall, handsome,
blonde treasurer of Heath Plastics
embezzles $100,000,000 from company
suspected of killing auditor
Do white people worry
that he's white –
I doubt it

Trade-offs

What is this guilt
you're trying to heap
upon me like bales of
cotton
No, life did not take
me into the fields
beside you
But I would gladly
carry your bales,
if you could bear
my griefs

Sixty-some Years

Sixty-some years
His rage beating at
her frail, washtub bent
body
Sixty-some years
Slowly, she rose
Walked over to the casket
Where lay her husband
Like linen for the
white folks, smoothed the
cover over him
Neatly folded those years
Sent them on with him

Back Home
After many years

What happened to this
street of my childhood
once pristine –
Solid, strong houses
brick, wooden, stucco
yellow, white – sun and
cloud colors
wrapping themselves around
us like warm blankets
The old home house gone
now, and with it
all our childhood secrets.
Others boarded up,
weather-bashed, graying,
skin peeling as if
touched by some scourge
Proud homes, they were
built by the first
generation out of slavery
Sitting here, now, like
old men, with empty
dreams.

Recycled Grief

She walked, head bent
small, thin body
clothed in the long
black mourning dress –
sallow, pale skin
creating a ghost
figure
A year she moved
through our house
like the shadow
of the one she
mourned
Eyes red from the
crying
The black period
over
she turned to gray
And wore it now
with only a few
brief tears
Then donned the
purple dress
allowing herself
an occasional smile

To a lady I knew in my childhood

I take my text from –

She walked in dignity down
the long church aisle
This diminutive woman
in a plain red dress
A rough straw sailor hat
complimenting the quiet
darkness of her face
Traces of Africa in
her speech
"Ah cum fum Chawston,"
she said, her voice soft
and light
"Y'all don' remember me.
Two yar ago, I walk in
here, dirty, hungry, homeless
The garbage pail my platter
The sidewalk my pillow
The deacon, whar' he?"
she said, looking over the
congregation, "I don' see
hum here. He give me
food. Church give me money
to get home to Chawston
and found me job."
Then she held up an envelope
"I cum to give back, so
you can give someone else

lying out there on the street
round your corner.
Now, let's all sing 'Reach
out and touch.'"
The song ended.
She walked back down the aisle
like a Nubian queen.

Harvesting
On a visit to Anne Spencer House
Lynchburg, Virginia   October 29, 1990

        Lady of the south winds we came to see you today, my sister and I, returning to this place we loved as children. The pungent smell of sweet shrub, in gentle Virginia winds, says home. Yet on the porch, waiting to enter, I think of Thomas Wolfe – and wonder.

        The door opens, we walk slowly, tentatively into – awesome stillness. Unsettled for a moment, pause, as if awaiting the warmth of your greeting. "My children from the north winds," you'd say.

        Chauncey, your only boy-child, understands we need this time – alone, stands back, lets us roam unaccompanied. We walk around touching the past. Everything the same, everything except the voices. No warm, soft drawl lingering in the air. No special words for each of us. The aura of you still here, though, and I want to whisper your name. My words consumed by penetrating silence.

        Aun' Tannie, we called you, knew your beauty as you knew the beauty of a leaf, a rose, a winter's sky. I see you in long, thick braids, leathery Indian complexion, wearing those daring Japanese pajamas, in a time of tight-corseted, Grant Wood women afraid to reveal their hunger for love, for sex, for free expression, or whatever the other natural needs of women are.

        But you, you sang of freedom, of love not stifled by time and gender. Your words, on the wind, found their way to the birds, the trees, the sky and even the "wee" spider. They understood their earth sister who spoke to them of beauty. As Cullen says of Keats, you too, "an apostle of beauty."

Quietly, we move around – this corner here, your love birds, Dumb, Belle and Stewed Prunes. Stewed Prunes, screwed up in a corner, mad. Dumb and Belle sitting close together on the perch. And who but you would have a crow, Old Black Joe, who could recite a phrase from Keats. And when he did not want to, cried, "I'm cold, I'm cold." Skeptics would say – a childhood fantasy, gone askew. No fantasy this, everyone in town knew Joe. What a place of wonder for a wide-eyed child, summers "back home" from the North.

So late this recognition of those who planted for the harvest, stray seeds, germinating in strange places long after the leaves have fallen. Your words a gift to me from Mama on my fourteenth birthday, Countee Cullen's *Caroling Dusk: An Anthology of Verse by Negro Poets*. I would sit for hours, savoring those words, touching them like precious stones. Yours and other Black poets', speaking to us like no one else had.

So late the recognition of the richness of those childhood moments when you would come to visit. Some of those same poets, whose words I touched, sitting around you in our parlor. We were brought in to meet them. Then Papa, who always feared our "tender" ears would hear something they should not, dismissed us, as he usually did, with a nod of the head. I would stay close by in the dining room listening to the voices of the Harlem Renaissance: Sterling Brown, James Weldon Johnson, Countee Cullen, Langston Hughes. I stand here in the center of you – remembering.

We walk into the sunroom. I see Uncle Ed graciously offering the adults "a little toddy," a glass of something smelling familiarly like a glass of something Papa called his medicinal whiskey. It was here, in this room, we listened to you and Mama laughing and talking about the arrogance and genius of Dubois, about the beauty of your roses, and about that *full freedom,* a term we heard often not understanding then, you speaking in poetry, Mama, in philosophical phrases. "North is an old narcissus," I heard you say once. Too big a concept for a child – so stored it away. Life revealed the meaning, the same bitter weeds growing in both soils, Mama digging at their roots in the North, you in the South.

   Rare friends, you and Mama, free spirits, found the common denominators, loved philosophy, freedom, humor, Dubois, James Weldon Johnson, Thoreau – and flowers. Defied the tight lady conventions of the time. While most early century women around you, drinking tea and tatting, you and Mama helping to organize the NAACP here and crying out against the hanging tree. Echo of your voices still in the fabric of this room.

   We move on upstairs into the room where hangs a painting by our younger sister, Dolly. *Cocktail Party,* she calls it. Everybody drinking scotch and grinning and grinning and drinking scotch. You loved it, said it portrayed the "uppityness of the Black bourgeoisie." You wanted the painting to remind whoever came your way, that "phonyness never wore a warm cloak."

   I look once more at the painting, then walk quickly into the adjoining room, our room when we visited. Sun streams in the window infusing me with the warmth of an earlier time. Bright chintz-covered beds (faded now like an aging beauty). We'd lie here in this field of multi-colored wild flowers straining to hear the words and laughter of adults in the room below.

I walk over to the window overlooking your garden – your garden, your sanctuary. A bird is singing out there. Didn't I see you turn to greet him? Then walk slowly through your roses, pluck the dead leaves? We'll join you there, walk through the rose garden with you.

Chauncey brings the key to your little garden house – *Edankrall*. We walk into a re-creation of the past. Pictures of you, Uncle Ed, your children – Bethel, Alroy, Chauncey, your grandchildren – and over there, Mama. The walls full of familiar. I stand at your writing desk feeling like an intruder. Only your Muses, Calliope and Euterpe, belong here watching over you as you create your poems.

We do not linger, go out by the lily pond, capture this day for bleaker times. There is a strong sense of your presence here in your garden. I listen for your words. Somewhere out there in the south winds. Have gathered them many times as you gather your roses. Your words about Browning and the beauty of Virginia, your words to the "gay little girl of the diving tank," your words to McSweeney of the Irish Rebellion, your words to a nasturtium, your words to the "wee" spider about freedom – but most of all – your words to me.

A sensitive, chubby, rosy-cheeked child with thick tangled hair. Ugly duckling – some called me. I, the Poroed, hot-combed one. "Poor lil' thing," they'd say. "Where'd she get all that bad hair?" But not you. Your greeting for me dispelled the hurt. Always the same. "Here come Jonathan's winter apples." And by your tone, I knew they, and I, must be very special.

Piece of Time

I once heard an old Alabama farmer say
"Everybody need a lil' piece a time a they own."

Each morning walking my dog
I find my place in the woods
A special place where I can
crawl inside myself, shed the old
skin from around my fringes
Coco understands, stretches out
quietly at my feet
Allowing me this moment
with other earth creatures

A green lizard there, up early,
sees us and freezes
I want to calm his fears and
say "I'm your earth sister"
He waits, then finds safety in a
nearby tree,
tall Carolina pine that
shimmers in the early morning
sunlight

I listen to my birds
The mockingbird singing his
tee-chow, tee-chow, tee-chow
changing to *chit-e-chow*
as we might change from
Bach to Basie
All sounds are joyous except
the *oo-a-coo-coo-coo* of
the mourning dove

Coco lifts a lazy eye
watching an indecisive butterfly
flutter from yellow jessamine
to wood violet
And an old possum sticks his
head up out of a patch of leaves
"Don't worry, old fella," I say
"I don't eat possum"
Untrusting, he skitters off
into the brush

The clouds speak softly to
me
One the shape of a cotton
cave I want to climb into
I watch them slowly shifting
changing, changing, changing –
infusing me with their gentle spirit
I can go home now
pull out the frying pan
and cook breakfast for my
family

Afterword

I've written practically all my life, it seems to me. But I'm *seriously* writing now. I write all the time – I get up writing. Things are in my head that I need to get up and put down. I didn't have that before. This is a wonderful period of my life as a writer. I was seventy-three when this period started.

I'm seventy-nine now. It's almost as if I'm trying to make up for lost time. My second husband was a writer, a beautiful writer, a journalist. Before I married him, I had had one short story published in John A. Williams' book, *Beyond the Angry Black* (Cooper Square Publishers, 1966), and that was all. My husband would always say, "I'm the writer in the family." And it stopped me. During that period I didn't write very much – it was almost like writing in the closet.

I kept my poems in a box and in a drawer for a long time. Toi Derricotte is the first poet who read my poems. My friend, Annie Laurie Tucker, with whom I exchanged poems said, "I think you should send Toi some of your poems to read." (Toi is her niece.) I said, "Oh I don't know. Take them out of the box and expose myself!" She insisted; she talked with Toi and Toi called me and said, "I'd like to see your poems." She took time to do a critique of each one. She said, "Read Sonia Sanchez for your political poems. Be sure you read Rita Dove. Have you read so and so?" She was so helpful.

It was Toi who said, "I want you to send in your works to Squaw [Valley Community of Writers.]" I guess I was the most surprised person to get accepted. Squaw was a wonderful experience – it was so open, everybody was so open. Galway Kinnell and Sharon Olds opened up the closed doors

Edited from a taped interview.

in my head. I felt like I could say whatever I wanted, whatever was deep down inside.

I also attended the Sandhills Writers Conference, held every year at Augusta College in Augusta, Georgia, where I met Laurence Lieberman, a wonderful critic. He read a poem of his at lunch about a bombed synagogue and a slave market on one of the Caribbean islands. It was striking. I went up to him afterward and said, "You know, I'm writing a poem about my grandmother's face that has to do with the slave market in Charleston." I told him what I was trying to do with it and he was quite interested. He inspired me to finish it.

Wherever I've gone to writers conferences, I've gotten that kind of help and encouragement. But I must say that Squaw was the greatest. When I was looking over my poems to select and send to you, many of them came out of Squaw or after Squaw.

* * * *

Family support has helped me a lot. I had a hard time thinking of myself as a writer. I thought of myself as a social worker and as a teacher. But my family keeps saying to me, "You're a writer." They've been encouraging to me.

You may not believe this, but when I was younger, I was very shy. Even in my high school yearbook, beside my name were the words "Seen – trying not to be." My sisters and I were quite different. Doll was always the bohemian, the really exciting kind of person that your parents and everybody else would say, "Well, you know, that's Doll" – which meant that she had license to do anything. And Rosemary was just sweet. But Carrie had license to do nothing! I felt that there was an expectancy of me to do the right thing all the time. And I'm so sorry I did the right thing too many times. I think I missed out on a lot of things that I could have risked, that might have been a little more exciting. But that is how I was. But in my writing I'm free. Oh yes, I'm real free.

I feel so open about it now. Squaw helped me with it some, but it must have been happening too – that I was becoming more open. And it also may be something of the times – people talk about more things than they used to. Now nobody can shut me up! I don't find any reason to shut down. I feel free to write on any subject now, even subjects I may have had trouble expressing openly before.

Maybe this happens with age. A friend of mine said to me, "You've got seventy-nine years of information packed in there. It'll come out." I guess that's part of it. There is a lot in there – and some of it is just opening up now. I feel a kind of urgency to keep on writing. You never know at any age, but certainly at this age you don't know what's going to happen tomorrow. In a sense that is an advantage because it keeps you going. I write more now, more consistently.

Writing is soothing to me. We all have our problems and instead of the problem weighting me down, I feel that writing eases it sometimes. There are times I wake up in the morning thinking about my son who has psychiatric problems. In the beginning, it consumed my thoughts. My son had his breakdown in 1974 and it's been an up-and-down situation, in and out of veterans' hospitals, sleeping on the streets of New York – I'd learn that after the fact. He was very creative, wrote beautiful, strong poetry and did lovely paintings – he still does lovely paintings. I don't think you ever get over what happens to your child of this nature, but you have to find ways of adjusting to it. I would have been a nervous wreck if I just kept giving in to it. But I found I could make myself move away from it through meditation and through my writing.

* * * *

A day never passes that I won't do some writing. Sometimes it's just revising something that I'm working on, or something will hit me – an old memory, and I'll want to write about that. It may be something that I see in the paper that I respond to. The poem, "I take my text from," came from something that happened in church. When I looked around and saw that woman coming down the aisle, I said to myself, she's from Charleston. And when she got up there, she said, "I come from Charleston." She just moved everybody. It was such a wonderful experience for everybody sitting there. She was with me – I took her home from church. I kept saying to myself *that* was the text of the day. This visiting minister didn't even comment on it. He took us off into something else that I don't even remember. But *that* was the text . If our regular minister had been there, I know he would have incorporated that in whatever text he had prepared. I was telling my sister about it and I said, "I'm going to write a poem and I'm going to call it, 'I take my text from.'" It was just before I went to Squaw and I wrote it there.

    The poem, I have a poem inside me, – Toi helped me in writing that. She kept saying, you need to write about your husband and your marriage. I remember how that poem came about. I was in Bob Hass's workshop on a Thursday at Squaw and we were all so tired – Thursday is a low point in the week of writing. Someone said, "I don't know how I'm going to write a poem for tomorrow." And I said, "I have a poem inside me that refuses to come out." And Hass said, "Write *that* for tomorrow." And next day when I was in Toi's workshop, I read it and I stopped and said, "Toi, *you* told me two or three years ago that I had to write about this." And she said, "It took a long time. Now keep on writing." And I will.

    I also want to write some very positive things about my second husband, because he was a very strong man. He started the first Black political party, the Progressive Democrats, back in the 1940's, which became a strong political force. He had a real fighting newspaper. Everybody says it's a wonder he wasn't lynched because of the kinds of things he would bring out in the paper. He did spend sixty days on a chain gang at that time for a trumped-up charge of libel, although he never used the name of the person in his story.

A white reporter wrote the same story and received no punishment. Everyone knew it was because my husband's political party was becoming too strong. The *New York Times* picked up the story and he became an international *cause celèbre*. But he was unafraid. I want to do some poems about that side of him too – that needs to be written.

I've written about growing up as a Black child in the North and in the South. Frankly there wasn't too much difference except that the South was warmer. Even though we were segregated in the South at that time, we didn't feel the segregation until we were older. As a child, you don't know that you're sitting in the back of the trolley car – your mama takes you to the back and you sit down. The real impact of Jim Crow came to me quite a bit later, when I was sixteen. I write about that in "My Grandmother's Leg."

I wrote about my mother in "At the Grave Site." My sisters and brothers had the same thought in 1935, when we were burying her, we've talked about this – here's Mama who integrated this town and yet here she is buried in the segregated section of the graveyard. It's hard enough to see your mother buried anyway, but to see *her* buried in the segregated section of the graveyard was very difficult.

She integrated the police department. She integrated the high school graduation line – Black students had to walk at the end of the line in Montclair, New Jersey. Mama had been up there many times about that. But when my sister Rosemary was getting ready to graduate, she went up there and she said, "We're not going to have this." This was one of her favorite expressions. She would always say that, whether it was the governor or the principal or the superintendent. She said, "My daughter's name is Rosemary Allen and this year we will have the line in alphabetical order." And sure enough they changed it and her daughter was up there in front.

She never passed, even in restaurants, though she could have. One time Mama was going into a restaurant in Newark and she took my brother Greg with her. Greg was very dark, smooth dark but with very straight hair. They didn't want to serve her unless she would say that Greg was East Indian. She spoke out loud and said, "No, we are Negroes and we're going to eat here as Negroes." She never raised her voice and hollered and yelled, but she would always have things together.

I got so much from my mother, I can see now at seventy-nine, looking back. She was the one who really introduced me to poetry . She bought us *A Child's Garden of Verse* and other little poetry books. And she would buy the poets of the Harlem Renaissance. We would read them and then I had to recite them – we always had to entertain the guests. Since I couldn't dance, I couldn't sing – my brother Bill could sing, my sister Doll could dance, Rose could play *Meditation* on the piano – my mother would have me reciting poetry.

* * * *

My major piece of work now is the story based on the life of my mother. I had thought of it as just the story of my mother. Then I went to a writer's workshop at Duke University and was told I was writing an historical novel. Shook me up a little bit. But when I thought about it, I thought, well – I've *done* all this historical research and my mother's father *was* a Confederate general.

I started writing this in the sixties. I was so angry with my mother's father – I didn't even know him of course. I never even thought of him as my grandfather. All I knew was that he was a Confederate general. I couldn't deal with that. He was always "my mother's father" and it stopped right there.

Since '86 everything has opened up for me in relation to that work. In 1990, when I went to Harrisonburg, Virginia, where my mother was born, the research librarian at James Madison University said to me, "Oh, there's a student here who would be so happy to meet you. He's been trying to find descendants of General Jones."

He called that evening and asked, "What is your connection with General Jones?" I said "I don't know that there's any connection with *this* General Jones." He asked, "What was your mother's mother's name?" I said, "Malinda Rice." He said, "Oh! Will you get upset if I tell you something?" I said "No, I'm searching truth, whatever the truth is." So he said, "I was in the courts the other day and I read that General Jones' second wife divorced him on the grounds of adultery with Malinda Rice." I said "Great!" He said, "What?" I said "Great. That does two things. It confirms for me that this *is* my mother's father." Notice I never said "my grandfather."

And the second thing – as a woman – when I think of all those southern white women who for years just allowed this, and all those young Black girls who were sexually abused – the powerlessness of women in what Mary Chestnut in her diary calls "that monstrous system," a system which continued long after the war – I think it was great that General Jones' second wife divorced him. From the young researcher, Dale Harter, I received a windfall of information on the General's family, going back to 1801 and on Malinda Rice's family, going back to the end of the 1700's. It would have taken me years to find all that. In fact, I had already been searching for years. My sister, Rosemary, travels with me, helps with the research. She has been wonderful through her support and encouragement.

My grandmother was born a slave in 1855 or '56. When she was thirteen, she had to go work as a maid with a Reverend Bowman and his wife who really looked out for her. When one of them died, she went to the Joneses as a maid and then a housekeeper. She was sixteen. General and Mrs. Jones had no children. He always wanted a child and of course his wife did too – she expressed that many times. But because of a long illness, this was not possible. What happened to Malinda happened to so many young Black girls during slavery and after the war.

I've done a great deal of research. I've read books on Black and white women on the slave plantation and after.

I've read all of Mary Chestnut and Black slave narratives to get some sense of what that relationship was. There was a bond between the Black woman and the white woman, and yet underneath there was suspicion and often certainly jealousy. Fortunately, General Jones' first wife was a very gentle, kind person. I learned this not from my mother but from my mother's dearest friend, Anne Spencer, a poet we called Aunt Annie. She told me about a porcelain-headed doll that General Jones' first wife had given my mother when she was a small child and a number of other little things that I never would have known, because it was sort of a taboo to even talk about it to your own children. The only thing we knew was that my mother's father was a Confederate general.

But he adored my mother. And she adored him. He taught her how to read. He taught her to learn to love poetry. He took her to many places that he didn't take her brother. It was a little upsetting to me to see that Uncle Billy wasn't treated the same as mother because he was brown – my mother was very fair. He took her into an ice cream parlor or restaurant, some place where Blacks could not go. He didn't hide that this was Malinda's child – most people in the town knew she was. The owner was very fond of my mother and would give her candy and everything. But one time someone in there whispered that this was "a little nigger bastard." My mother's father overheard and went over and knocked the man out.

After I realized what he had done, I had a metamorphosis of feeling about him. He gave land and money for the first Black church there. He gave money to the Black school for ex-slaves and their children. When Malinda died, he had another Black mistress. And he left all of his estate to the second Black mistress.

I'm taking a genealogy course at the Shepherd's Center for Senior Citizens in Columbia, South Carolina – they've done a lot on the Civil War. I wanted to include his Army career, what he did in the war. There was a lot of question about whether he was a coward or a hero; some said he was a coward because his leg was hurt but not too bad. One letter I saw about Civil War generals who lived in that area gave his Army career record and things he had done that were very popular. But it said that after the war he was "a disgrace to himself and to the community." It said he had gotten connected to a Black woman. And it said, "Strike him off the list. And be sure to do it in black, with great big letters: BLACK."

I'm also trying to include what it was like for my mother. You're in neither world really – that is a very difficult position to be in. When I said there was too much anger in me in the sixties, well some of that anger remains. I have a character, Uncle John, in the novel who is still angry at the general. That's Malinda's brother, an ex-slave, a very strong man. I want to keep some of that anger for him. I couldn't just write a sweet syrupy story about the general. I had to have these two sides.

* * * *

I have three pieces that I really want to finish: the story of my mother; a series of stories about the courtyard between two brownstone houses in Brooklyn where I lived for a time – I call it "The Court;" and a poem about Ota Benga. Ota Benga was brought over here in 1904 with five other pygmies. That was a time when scientists were looking for "the missing link." Ota and the others were exhibited at the World's Fair in St Louis in 1904. Later, he was exhibited in a cage in the Bronx zoo – I can't remember whether it was a baboon or an orangutan's cage. People flocked to see him. Black ministers became incensed. My older brother Hunter's father, who was chairman of the education committee of the National Black Baptist Convention, was contacted to see what to do about Ota.

Ota Benga lived in our home. It's conceivable that my mother taught him whatever English he knew or whatever things within the home you would teach a person. I don't remember much about him except that down at the end of the hall was this nice gentle man. Hunter remembers that he would tell stories about the animals in Africa, he would flap his arms like a bird if he was telling us about a bird, he would act things out.

I had not thought about doing a poem about Ota – I thought of him as part of the story about my mother. But two summers ago at Squaw, I told C. K. Williams that I had started a poem the night before about Ota, but that I didn't have the information – I really needed to do a lot of research. C. K. Williams was very much interested in it and said, "Well Carrie, when you do this, I'd like you to send it to me as you go along. I will do a critique on it and help you with it." I'm just delighted that he made that offer.

In the beginning it was just the joy of writing. Now I would really like to pass it on. I feel that people should know some of these things. I said one time that if a publisher does not pick up the book about my mother that it's important to leave it even to the family. So I guess I have moved from just the joy of writing and keeping things in a box and in a drawer to really wanting to share some things.

Available from Chicory Blue Press

Crimson Edge Chapbooks:

Late Afternoon Woman, *poems,* by Sondra Zeidenstein.

Piece of Time, *poems,* by Carrie Allen McCray.

Full Moon, *stories,* by Tema Nason.

Unveiling, *poems,* by Rita Kiefer.

Sellie and Dee: A Friendship, *memoir,* by Estelle Leontief.

Chapbooks are $7.95 each.

Other Chicory Blue Press titles:

A Wider Giving: Women Writing after a Long Silence, ed. by Sondra Zeidenstein, $14.95.

Memoir, poems by Honor Moore, $11.95.

Heart of the Flower: Poems for the Sensuous Gardener, ed. by Sondra Zeidenstein, $13.95.

Order from:

Chicory Blue Press, 795 East Street North, Goshen, CT 06756 (203) 491-2271.

Add $1.75 for the first book and $.50 for each additional book.

Connecticut residents, please add sales tax.